INTRODUCTION

The genteel town of Marlborou
is a prosperous market town t
gives a sense of ineffable w
being. Its High Street, one of
widest in the UK, moves slov
with late-registration cars ambling
past a gallery of frock shops and
coffee bars housed in period
buildings. Timber frames and
hanging tiles predominate, with
only occasional modern
structures blending seamlessly
with more ancient neighbours.

Fed by the clear waters of the
freshly-risen River Kennet,
Marlborough was where the
Saxons and Celts made their first,
tentative moves from the Neolithic
Age to settled life and agriculture.
In Norman days, it became an
important fortified centre and for
much of the Middle Ages was
home to a mighty sprawling
castle.

changing
d into 700
line. The
vamp that
s drained
being, and
city in the
west. The castle fell out of favour
and into ruins, and though
Marlborough was still, up until the
seventeenth century, the second
biggest town in Wiltshire its role
was changing, becoming little
more than a prosperous coaching
station servicing horse-born
traffic between London and Bath.
It was soon to lose even this.

When canals were dug to link
these two cities, the rolling
topography saw the new
important waterways bypass
Marlborough by several miles.
When the railways were planned,
a major local landowner objected
to a line through the Marlborough
Downs and the route through

North side of the High Street

Swindon was chosen instead. The M4 was also to follow this more northerly passage and the ancient A4, from London to Marlborough, lost its strategic role. The largest coaching inn became a school – albeit quite a successful one – and the town rather lost its position at the heart of progress.

Afterthought rail links – through a spur on a spur – never thrived and Marlborough withered on the edge of the UK's transport links. Finally, the line was discontinued.

Which leaves the Marlborough of today. The castle is now little more than a mound, marooned in the private preserve of Marlborough College and closed to visitors. All that remains are traditions dating back more than a thousand years, a private school with an enviable reputation and a certain provincial charm. And, thanks to a seventeenth-century fire that destroyed a line of shacks in the middle of the High Street, plenty of parking.

But perhaps its isolation has also acted in Marlborough's favour. Sidelined by the major transport links, the town was free to relax, and to resist much of the urbanisation that would otherwise have followed. Marlborough never wanted to become Swindon – freestanding telegraph poles have been firmly banned on the High Street – and the town has charted its own course into a genteel provincial backwater.

Marlborough today is an enviable place to live and is also a surprisingly rewarding town to visit.

High Street

MERLIN'S BOROUGH?

The origins of Marlborough's name are lost in the swirls of time, but the most appealing explanation is that it is a corrupted version of 'Merlin's Barrow' (Merlin's grave), 'Merlin's Borough' (Merlin's mound) or Merlin's burgh (Merlin's stronghold). These make perfect sense if you accept the myth that the Marlborough Mound (see page 4) was where King Arthur's legendary wizard was interred.

This is not completely backed up by historical evidence. For a start, there are not thought to be any bones in the Mound – and people have looked. The original legend of Merlin described a wild-man prophet who roamed the moors of Wales in the sixth century AD while the Mound has been dated back to Neolithic times, thousands of years earlier. By the sixth century, such a significant man-made landmark must presumably have already had a name.

In fact, we know it did. Ancient records already list a bewildering range of options that clearly foreshadow the current Marlborough. Through the ages it has been variously spelt Marleberg, Marleberge, Malbrow, Marleborrow, Marleburgh, Merleberg, Merlberge, Marlebyri, Marlensborrow, Mierleb, Marlingsboroe, Merleberga, Mierlbi, Merleberg, Merligsboroe, Marleborough, Mrllgei, Marleeborow, Marlbrough, Marlebor, Marlbury, Merlebury, Marlee-borowe, Marleboarough, Marle-borought, Morlebrougth, Marleburgh (meaning Chalk Town), Mearleah (meaning cattle boundary) and Marlesbeorg.

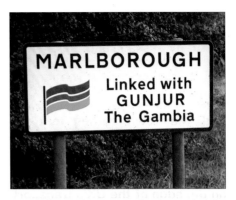

When the town had a mint in AD 1072, the spelling used on local coinage was Maerlebi.

The Merlin myth was certainly current from the thirteenth century onwards. The town's coat of arms, devised in the nineteenth century, affirms the connection with its motto 'Ubi nunc sapientis ossa Merlini' (Where now are the bones of wise Merlin); there's a Merlin Hotel and several of the junior football teams play under the name 'Marlborough Merlins'. The theory is plausible at least.

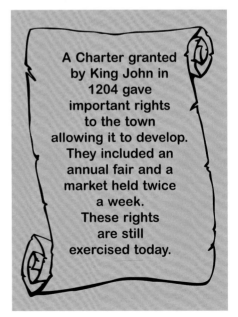

A Charter granted by King John in 1204 gave important rights to the town allowing it to develop. They included an annual fair and a market held twice a week. These rights are still exercised today.

Marlborough Mound in College Grounds

MARLBOROUGH MOUND

Though one of Europe's major Neolithic monuments, Marlborough Mound is firmly in private ownership. It is hemmed in on every side by the buildings of Marlborough College, barely signposted and certainly not open to the public.

The Mound is nineteen metres high and its base would comfortably cover a football field. The slope is steeper than Silbury Hill five miles to the west but it certainly dates back to the same time, at the very birth of civilisation. Recent coring of Marlborough Mound produced four charcoal samples from different levels and radiocarbon dating placed construction fairly precisely in the years around 2400 BC. This means we now know

> It has been suggested that the spiral path is a 17th century re-cut of an original Neolithic feature.

when it was built, though it is still not known why.

These two Neolithic mounds are connected by more than just age. Silbury Hill is very near the source of the River Kennet which, by the time it passes Marlborough Mound, is already a significant waterway, tinkling with the cool clear waters that are common with chalk streams. It is quite understandable why this should have quickly become a permanent settlement at a time when nomadic hunter-gatherers were starting to set roots. Nineteen metres might not appear especially high but it sounds better expressed in Imperial measures; it's more than 62 feet to the summit. Once you approach, its scale becomes much more imposing, and the climb itself is a (modest) challenge. It's certainly worth the effort. Seventeenth-century landscaping introduced a circular walkway that spiralled upwards, taking four circuits to reach the top, and a belvedere to make the most of the views.

The Mound has more recently been used by Marlborough College. It housed a water tank on the summit, which must have given them excellent water pressure, but this has been cleared away. For many years, the school used part of the Neolithic moat for its swimming pool, which followed its ancient curve, though this has now been filled and covered.

Silbury Hill

The top of the hill is round and flat, with a slight depression in the middle, giving the impression of a ring doughnut, but one that's 30 metres across. It's an atmospheric place to stroll around but currently overgrown with trees. It is hotly debated whether these trees are destroying or preserving the structure and the current policy is only to cut those down that are likely to cause imminent damage. For now, they mean that views from the summit are restricted to enchanting glimpses of the town's skyline, from church spires to serried tiles, that can't be seen from any other vantage point.

Finding a clear view of the Mound is not easy. It can be seen from the steps of the town hall, where the summit can be glimpsed across the town to the left of St Peter's Church, or from Granham Hill as you head in from Pewsey. The best views are from the top of St Peter's Church tower, open to visitors on Saturdays, while the closest you can officially approach is along the A4 heading out of town just beyond the College, where the Mound is about 200m to the south.

Marlborough Mound by Colt Hoare 1812

THE CASTLE

In its heyday, the Castle would have been huge. Simply because there is so little left it is easy to forget that Marlborough Castle was able to accommodate the full royal entourage of what was a rich and extensive kingdom.

It wasn't until the Norman invasion of 1066 that Marlborough Castle came into being as a fairly modest fortification teetering on top of Marlborough Mound. When William the Conqueror took control of the Marlborough area in 1067, he set Roger, Bishop of Salisbury, to build a wooden motte and bailey castle. By 1070, this was substantial enough to serve as a prison for Ethelric, Bishop of Selsey. Ethelric was an important leader of the resistance to Norman rule, and died in captivity. At the same time, a mint was established in Marlborough that was to issue currency through the reigns of both Williams I and II.

> The Statute of Marlborough was passed by Henry III in 1267. It is the oldest piece of legislation still in force in the United Kingdom.

By 1080, the Castle was suitable to accommodate a King, and King William was a frequent visitor. He was very taken with Savernake Forest, where he "loved the tall deer as if he were their father" but, rather worryingly for any children, hunted and ate them at every opportunity. For the next 500 years, the castle would remain under the ownership of the crown and frequently played host to the court.

King Henry I kept Easter at Marlborough Castle in 1110. In the Civil War, it was held for Matilda against Stephen, and was then given by Richard I (Coeur de Lion)

Marlborough Castle

Marlborough Castle

to his brother (and later King) John, who married at the Castle and established his treasury here. It was the castle John favoured most during his reign and was where his son, the young Henry III, spent much of his childhood.

Its most significant moment in history was perhaps under Henry III, when it was where the Statute of Marlborough was signed. In many ways, the Statute of Marlborough was more important than Magna Carta, which had just given rights to the baronial class. The Statute of Marlborough gave rights to smaller landowners and limited the royal right to take possession of property in the event of the owner's death. This came too late for many of the locals and even now much of the land around Marlborough remains in the possession of the Crown.

Perhaps being forced to make this concession changed the Royals' attitude to Marlborough, because quite suddenly the palace fell out of favour. Though the Castle remained in royal ownership, it was used as a dower house for Queen Eleanor, who lived out her widowhood here. It is not known what role it played in the War of the Roses – though Edward IV was certainly there at some point – but in the straitened years that followed and with the advent of explosives, it lost its strategic importance. By 1403, the castle, along with its many chapels, gatehouses and outer baileys were in ruins, its stones enthusiastically scavenged to build St Peter's Church and some of the town.

King John

7

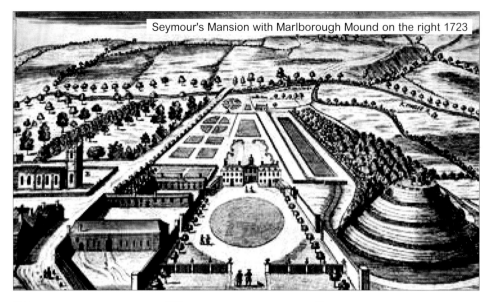

Seymour's Mansion with Marlborough Mound on the right 1723

MARLBOROUGH THROUGH THE AGES

In the years that followed its 1204 Royal Charter, Marlborough grew; churches were enlarged at either end of the town: grave-shaped St Peter's for the High Street and St Mary's at The Green. The castle was given to the Seymour family who built a mansion in its grounds. Mills, both for grain and cloth, were built along the river and the town quietly prospered.

It still preserved some royal favour. Cardinal Wolsey was ordained here before moving up to Hampton Court to run the country, while Henry VIII spent plenty of time hunting deer in Savernake and courting Jane Seymour.

Elizabeth I granted Marlborough a further charter of incorporation but a century later, when the Civil War came to town, Marlborough firmly supported Parliament. In 1642, it was overrun by Royalist troops from Oxford and 120 prisoners, including the town's MP, were led off in irons.

Structural damage came in 1653, when a fire started in a tanner's yard near to what is now the Wellington Arms. Fanned by a southerly wind, flames swept through the Shambles, a selection of hovels, shops and market stalls that huddled in the middle of what is now the High Street. Sparks caught the thatched roofs of the more elegant buildings on either side, the Town Hall and the fire spread up to The Green. In all, 250 houses, much of the town, ended up being destroyed.

Oliver Cromwell, by then Lord Protector, rewarded Marlborough's early support for Parliament by organising a national subscription

> **The Great Fire in 1653 destroyed many of the buildings in the High Street.**

8

to rebuild the town. Marlborough swung back into business in just a few years. The town centre traders were limited to the twice-weekly gatherings authorised by King John's ancient charter and were never again allowed to build their stalls into permanent shambles. The 1653 fire does much to explain the generously broad High Street of Marlborough today.

That wasn't the end for Marlborough and fire. Major blazes happened in 1679 and then again in 1690. Marlborough's carelessness was noticed in Parliament, which decided it was time to hand down some advice. An act was passed "to prohibit the covering of houses and other buildings with thatch or straw in the town of Marlborough." And this was vigorously enforced; even now the few thatched houses that can be seen in Marlborough were outside the strict borough boundaries of that time.

The diarist Samuel Pepys visited Marlborough on the 15th of June 1668, when the town was newly rebuilt after the fire. "Before night came to Marlborough, and lay at the 'Hart'; a good house and a pretty fair town for a street or two: and what is most singular is, their houses on one side having their penthouses supported with pillars, which makes it a good walk."

Pepys treated himself to "supper and music whose innocence pleased me" and two menus from his hotel, the White Hart, remain from the period so we can glimpse what he might have eaten. One offers: 'Supper. Mottton rost and boyled, capons and pullets, rabitts, sugar, milke, sallets, etc.', and another: 'Supper. Calves' heads, a piece of beefe, marye bones, plovers, partiges, pyes, crème, sucketts, and comfates and other delicacies'. Pepys slept so well that "all of the five coaches that came this day from Bath were gone out of the town" before he

Chandler's Yard where Royalist troops may have entered the town

awoke. A Blue Plaque on 114 High Street commemorates his stay.

Through the 1700s, Marlborough thrived on its location, midway between London and Bath. Turnpikes were introduced all along the A4 and in 1784 the road was chosen for the first Royal Mail coach route. The Seymours' mansion was turned into a luxurious coaching inn and was said to be the finest on the London to Bath route. By 1770, a golden era of easy money had started to flow through the town. The Crown Hotel, The Lamb Inn and the Castle & Ball Hotel are just a few places that still have distinctive features for carriages and stabling. Taverns, hotels and hostelries boomed.

With this came crime. There was a gibbet at Gallows Close, often used for burglars or deserters, a set of stocks by the Town Hall steps that were in use until 1825 and a pillory. A newly-

> The town became a popular stopping place halfway between Bath and London.

established newspaper, the Marlborough Journal, lists some of the offences. It records that in 1773 "Edward Messenger stood an hour in the pillory in this town, in pursuance of the statute, for having in his custody several pieces of venison." There was also a whipping post and as the whipper had to be paid, a record was kept by the authorities. In one day in 1771, no fewer than five people were whipped: two for stealing iron, another for appropriating a brass pot, the fourth for converting some butter to his own use, while the fifth was found with his hand in another man's pocket.

Local sports included horse racing and also another traditional game that is less familiar,

Thatched cottages in George Lane

The Ducking Stool

described in 'The Scouring of the White Horse', a rambling travel book by the Victorian clerk Tom Hughes:

"On Tuesday the 28th of September, 1773, one guinea will be given to be played for at Backsword, which shall be adjudged to the Man who breaks most heads; and eight men breaking eight heads shall receive 5s each. The blood to run one inch or deemed no head."

On a domestic note, there was also a ducking stool that was used to punish 'common scolds'. This was a wooden stool attached to a large beam and mounted on wheels. Offending women (and it was only women) would be strapped to the chair, wheeled around town and then rolled to the bottom of Granham Hill to be dunked in the river.

The Town Hall stocks are preserved in the old cells beneath the building.

This bucolic world soon came to an end. The 1810 Kennet and Avon Canal formed a new water link between Bath and Reading and therefore the Thames; it skirted close to Marlborough but went instead through Devizes which rapidly grew to become the larger town. More seriously, in 1840 the Great Western Railway chose a route through Swindon, 12 miles to the north. Swindon expanded; Marlborough shrank. Trains were far more comfortable than rickety horse-drawn carriages and the lucrative coaching trade collapsed.

Marlborough started to lose influence too. It was a fairly rotten borough, returning two members of Parliament despite having a relatively small population, and scraped through the reforms of 1831 with both MPs in post. But in 1867, its quota was cut to one MP and in 1885 the ward was abolished. Since then, Marlborough has voted as a part of the constituency of Devizes.

Town Hall

THE HIGH STREET

Flanked by The Green on one side and The Parade on the other, Marlborough Town Hall gazes majestically over the High Street and provides a natural focus. From its steps, views reach along the High Street, which curves gently as it follows the ancient flood-limit of the River Kennet. The sheer width of the High Street, the second-widest in the UK, means that despite the curve you can still see clearly to St Peter's Church at the College end of town and the Marlborough Mound beyond.

The Town Hall itself has been rebuilt several times and its current incarnation is Victorian, built in the 'Dutch' style and completed in 1902. The

> The Green Dragon opened in 1650 and is the oldest pub still trading.

south-facing buildings from here are some of the best-preserved timber-framed buildings, still with the second-floor penthouse rooms and galleried walkways described by Samuel Pepys. Every so often, the houses are separated by narrow walkways that thread up towards Back Lane and Marlborough Common, high above the town. Once, these alleys allowed in the royalist soldiers of the seventeenth century Civil War but their names - Chandler's Yard, Ironmonger's Yard - hint at more modest intentions.

Wider alleyways head south towards the river: Angel Yard is newly-built and lined with offices and Hillier's Yard leads down to more shops, parking and the Kennet. Alma Yard is perhaps the prettiest, lined with private houses and colourful town gardens.

The twice-weekly market runs from the Town Hall as far as the

Castle & Ball Hotel, halfway along the High Street, where Marlborough Castle's jurisdiction began; beyond this, the buildings were primarily residential. Not now. Shops run the length of the High Street and up around the crescent of Hughenden Yard. The retail frenzy calms gradually as the High Street reaches the redundant Church of St Peter and St Paul. The church now contains a craft shop as well as being one of more than 30 outlets serving coffee in the town.

While many English town centres have seen commercial life bleed away into out-of-town shopping centres, Marlborough has thrived. There are charity shops, of course, but even these tend to be quite upmarket. National chains are present but generally Marlborough seems to nurture individual, boutique outlets, serving specialised interests with considerable skill.

Marlborough's shops are impressive. Clothes shops range from vintage to designer, and a number of jewellers showcase a range of styles and prices. There are barbers that provide wet shaves and fast cuts and hairdressing salons that devote hours to colour and design. The essentials are all present, with butchers, bakers, haberdashers and hardware shops, but also more unusual outlets. There is a sports outfitter that supplies top-end equipment as well as sportswear for both the College and the state school. A bookshop sells art equipment, and a record shop that draws major-league musicians to the town for impromptu concerts.

In other towns, so wide a high street might be turned into a highway. Not in Marlborough. Parking on both sides and in the middle slows the traffic down to a pedestrian-friendly crawl; cars give way to people. A constant stream of visitors throngs the pavements and the atmosphere is invariably lively and cheerful.

The Polly Tea Rooms

THE MERCHANT'S HOUSE

After the great fire of 1653, the Merchant's House was one of the first to take advantage of Cromwell's reconstruction fund – and with one of the largest claims.

It belonged to Thomas Bayly, a silk merchant, but the family wealth did not survive for too many generations and the building was rapidly subdivided. A through-passage was installed, dividing the main shop into two units and by 1731 the building was divided into seven tenancies, including a surgeon, a saddler, an ironmonger and two coopers. From then, it was variously home to the Marlborough Journal, the town's first newspaper, along with a succession of printers, stationers and druggists. One half was let to WH Smiths for a number of years until they moved to a larger property further up the street. In 1991, the Merchant's House was bought by the Town Council, who leased it to a charity to be restored to its former original state. Now, although the eastern section of the divided shopfront is still rented out as retail, the western section has re-opened as the Merchant's House's own shop. The rest of the property, including two upper stories, is being painstakingly restored back to its seventeenth-century state.

At first glance, the shop seems like several other Marlborough retail outlets. A selection of handicrafts, ceramics, decorative glassware and picture-frames form an eclectic range of inessentials. Sign up for one of the guided tours, however, and you'll get to see the rest of the interior, beautifully restored, and the decorative gardens behind.

The most original room in the house is on the first floor,

The House is leased from the Council for a peppercorn rent - literally a bag of peppercorns!

The Merchant's House

The Panelled Chamber

known as the Panelled Chamber. Later, divisions have been removed and the floor, wall panelling, fireplace and overmantle are all original. The oak panelling on the walls is pegged in place without glue, the limestone fireplace probably came from Swindon and a stained glass sundial, used for setting clocks and watches, was probably supplied by John Oliver of London. Thanks to the structural disruption caused by adding the ground-level walkway, the floor is uneven and there is a decisive hump in the middle of the span but it's a glorious room filled with light from the large windows, galleried out over the pavement below.

The homes of today centre on the kitchen and that was also true back then, though it would be the servants that gave it life and bustle. It is still possible to catch a wisp of the kitchen's former glory, with a floor of Dorset stone, an Elizabethan ventilated oak food cupboard and a 1690 lantern clock. The owners would dine more formally upstairs in the dining room, also known as the Painted Chamber. This has been beautifully restored to the original colour-scheme, painted vertical stripes over a dark green background. The overall effect is remarkably forceful compared to the milder colours of today's pastel age.

There's something of interest everywhere you look. All the furniture, tapestries and art works are of the period. In one of the servant's bedrooms, there is a traditional bed where the mattress is supported on a lattice of rope. This explains the phrase 'sleep tight'; the ropes would have to be tightened every night.

Guided tours of the Merchant's House, 132/133 High Street are run on Tuesday, Friday and Saturday from 10:30-15:00 from April to October.

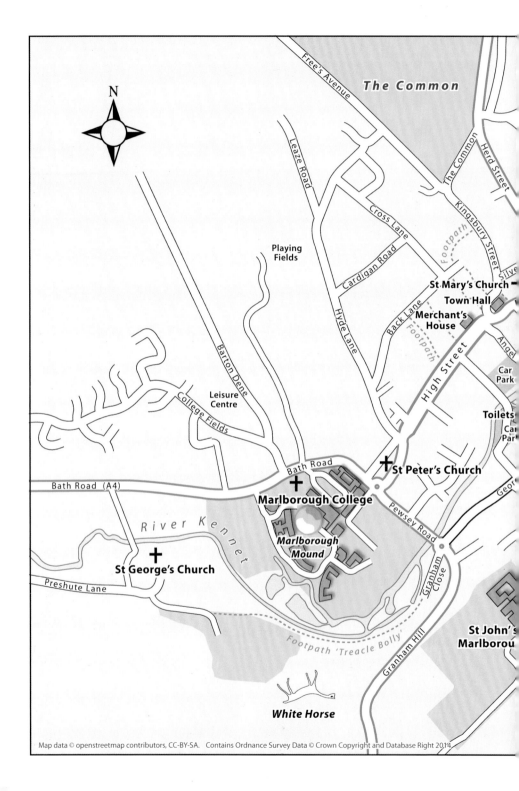

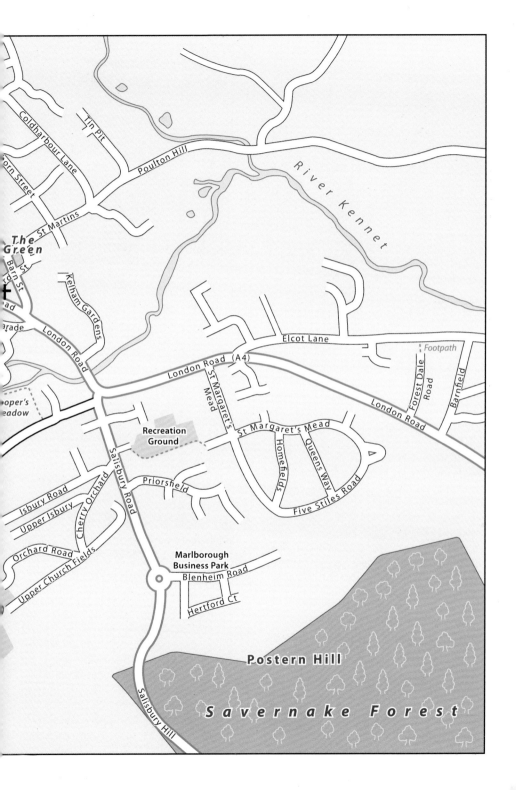

The Parade

© Duravitski / Alamy

THE PARADE

Until New Road was built in 1812, all traffic from the south-east into the High Street came up The Parade, the only part of town to completely escape the 1653 fire.

Unsurprisingly, these houses are some of the oldest buildings. Two of these are found at the upper part of The Parade on the western side. They wear their years lightly but are built with

Coat of Arms on no. 15

cruck trusses. This form of timber framing involved finding a suitably curved tree and splitting it in half; this gives two symmetrical bits of timber that can be used to make the frame.

The building that is now the art gallery of Katharine House in the lower part of The Parade can also be dated by the close-beam construction of its roof. For at least 250 years, this was a working rope factory until it closed in 1965. The roof timbers are closely spaced, a lavish use of timber not known in Wiltshire in any building later than 1588. In that year, the threat of the Spanish Armada meant that all sizeable trees were requisitioned to build naval vessels and never again would wood be so prolifically available. Two Elizabethan windows and some shoes found in the attic confirmed the building's age.

Though it used to be the main route into the town from the south, The Parade was never satisfactory for horse-drawn traffic. The lower part where it opened out into the triangular Kennet Place (now more parking) in front of the Rope Works would often get so muddy it was known as 'The Swamp'. The horses would then have to pull the carriages up a very steep incline – and coming down was worse. For this reason, the town carved New Road through the landscape, leaving St Mary's at the top of a high rampart wall.

Today, the best reason to venture down to this part of town is to shop for arts and antiques. The Marlborough Parade Antiques Centre is an Aladdin's cave. This former chapel provides a trading post for what must be approaching 30 traders who sublet small areas. Each is packed with a huge variety of collectibles: display cabinets,

Katharine House

walls and floors are all filled and covered. It's easy to lose hours in here. More modern exhibits are more elegantly displayed at the charming Katharine House Gallery, housed in the oldest part of the former rope factory that specialises in contemporary art and sculpture. The area around the back, that once housed the more industrial parts of the rope factory, sells more antiques and larger items of furniture.

The Parade used to be called
'The Marsh' but was known
locally as 'The Swamp'.

Antiques Centre

THE GREEN

It has often been said that the part of Marlborough around The Green started as a Saxon settlement, with Normans at the other end of the High Street around the Castle gates. There's no great evidence for this but this end of town does maintain a slightly different character. The Green was traditionally home to the annual Sheep Fair but in 1893 this was moved to the Common.

Now The Green is a pretty little area of trees and benches, only slightly marred by the busy road to Swindon heading north through its heart. On the north, a rather grand set of eighteenth- and nineteenth-century buildings bask in the midday sun along Silverless Street. This used to be the town's Jewish quarter till they were expelled in 1275. Heading east, St Martin's has a line of five very typical terraced houses, with tile-hanging, jettying, false timber-framing and oriel windows. Where

The avenue of lime trees is nearly two hundred years old.

Oxford Street runs off The Green, there is a Methodist Church on the spot where John Wesley preached in 1745 and 1747 but the church wasn't built until 1816 and the current incarnation dates back to 1910. The prettiest aspect is perhaps to the west of The Green, where sixteenth- and seventeenth-century cottages back on to St Mary's Courtyard; number 29 was William Golding's family home and has a plaque.

There are two ways back to the High Street; down Kingsbury Street, travelling under the overhanging tiled porch of Dormy House, or taking a detour around St Mary's Church. The two routes meet at the top of Perrins Hill, an ancient paved pathway with steps down to the back of the Town Hall to The Parade.

The Green

Marlborough College

© Mark Draisey / Alamy

THE COLLEGE

The collapse of the coaching trade had one good result; Marlborough College was founded. The Castle Mansion, built by the Seymours on the site of the Castle, had been operating as the Castle Inn. This had become the smartest overnight stop on the London to Bath route, and at its peak changed up to 40 carriages a night, had beds for sixty guests and more than sixty horses for travellers. When the coaches stopped, the Castle Inn hit hard times. Its trade had gone and its lease was running out. At the time, a group of clergymen, supported by William Gladstone among others, were trying to establish a private school for "the sons of the poorer professional classes and sons of clergymen of the Established Church." Their aim was to provide a good education at an affordable price. In 1842,

they picked the Castle Inn as the ideal site for this new establishment. In 1843, the Castle Inn re-opened as Marlborough College; the annual fees were 30 guineas for the sons of clergyman and 50 guineas for lay students. The first intake of 200 students quickly swelled and five years later Marlborough was the second largest private school in England; only Eton was larger.

Eight years on, the school almost closed again. The original school ignored organised sports, and the students spent their spare time poaching in the forest and river and generally running wild. In a period known as 'The Great Rebellion', battles opened up between the students and the school authorities. This came to a climax in the winter of 1851 when there was a four-day strike and a week of anarchy and vandalism; the founding headmaster resigned and reform was inevitable.

Covered Bridge & Porter's Lodge

Marlborough College's ambition had always been to rival established schools such as Winchester or Rugby, and its new headmaster was chosen from the latter; Dr Cotton, Assistant Master at Rugby, was appointed in 1852. The boys were distributed into houses, playing fields were laid out and organised games established. Cricket and rugby were introduced in 1853 and hockey in 1874.

There were a few difficult years. News of the rebellion had spread and student numbers dropped; in 1855, it had just 340 children. More established schools had a network of endowments that could be called

Marlborough Summer School has become hugely popular with locals and visitors alike.

upon when times got hard; not so newly-opened Marlborough. There was talk of merging with the town's Grammar School, itself dating back to 1550, but the townspeople turned it down "being in any way identified with that bankrupt institution on the Bath Road."

It was the Grammar School that struggled, however, closing briefly on two occasions and even applying to merge with the College. By this time, Marlborough College had rebuilt its reputation and turned down their offer. Over the years, the College rose up the ranks of the great public schools.

Marlborough College has continued to develop. Games fields have been ironed on the landscape all around the west and north of town. The banana-shaped swimming pool that once made use of the Marlborough Mound's

Neolithic moat has gone, and today its Olympic-sized pool indicates the improved level of facilities. Although it has long abandoned any claims to be affordable, Marlborough College is now generally recognised as one of the UK's leading public schools with a reputation for turning out students who, at the very least, are 'nice'. John Betjeman is one of many notable Marlburians, and his comfortable vision of England somehow seems natural for a school that bestows an effortless self-confidence on all its students. Other alumni include Bruce Chatwin, Siegfried Sassoon, James Mason, Nick Drake, William Morris, Chris de Burgh, Ernest Thesiger, Christopher Martin-Jenkins and Mark Tully.

In a nod to the modern age, Marlborough College introduced older girl students in the sixth form in 1968, allowing them through the full curriculum in 1989. Since then, it has rapidly acquired a reputation for turning out a number of well-connected women. So far it has provided the Duchess of Cambridge (and her sister), Samantha Cameron, Frances Osborne, Sally Bercow and many more carefully-bred political consorts. To balance things out, the school also groomed Mark Phillips to marry Princess Anne.

You don't need to be a full-time student to get a taste of a Marlborough education. Since 1975, the College has run a residential Summer School, making use of the buildings while the students are on holiday. This means you'll get to climb the Mound, visit the rather elegant chapel and attend some of the extensive range of courses whatever your age.

Originally Seymour's Mansion, now Marlborough College

© Trevor Payne / Alamy

23

CHURCHES

By 1223, the three churches of Marlborough were established as St Mary's, St Peter's and Preshute. But only parts of today's buildings can still be dated back to that period.

The Green was served by St Mary's Church, reached by an alley leading off the eastern end of the High Street and standing over a sheer drop onto New Road. The fire of 1653 took out the roof and the interior and even the stone sections had to be seriously rebuilt as the Norman arcades became unstable.

Reconstruction, under Cromwell, would have come with conditions. In Puritan style, the interior would be austere and the chancel would not be replaced. Over the centuries, various amendments were made – galleries were built, aisles were moved – and today it has a

somewhat lopsided interior. It does have an interesting defaced Roman relief of the goddess Fortuna dating back to AD 300. Presumably, this was brought over from the Roman settlement of Cunetio two miles downstream.

St Peter's Church is at the College end of the High Street. This was built using stones from the castle in 1460 on the site of an earlier chapel and is where Cardinal Wolsey was ordained. It was also upwind of Marlborough's great fire of 1653 and it escaped unharmed.

A major reconstruction in 1863 stopped St Peter's falling down, but it also changed its character and in 1974 the church was declared redundant. Freed of

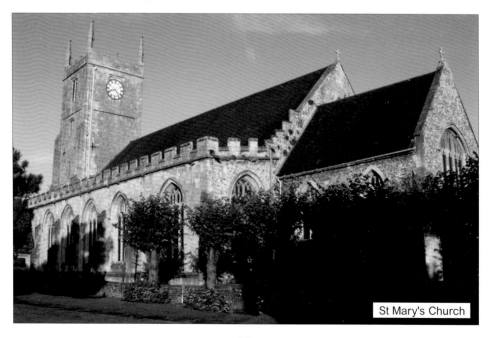

St Mary's Church

St Peter's Church

its religious obligations, it is now a spacious and spectacular coffee outlet with a large display of arts and crafts.

On Saturdays, guided tours go up St Peter's Church tower. The narrow winding staircase (137 steps) leads up past a small historic exhibition that includes a set of stocks that once held Cardinal Wolsey, who when young got drunk and abused a local bigwig. It also passes the curfew bell that was rung every night at 8pm. Deriving from the French couvre-feux, this was the time when every resident had to be at home, covering their fires, and presumably dates back to a Norman edict. This bell was rung – and curfew observed – right up until the First World War.

> The black font in St George's Church may have been used to baptise King John's family.

Historically, the most important church in Marlborough was to the west of the town in Preshute, first registered in 1186. Marooned in the fields by the disappearance of the castle, St George's Church is beautifully set on a chalkland slope with the River Kennet burbling close by. Its font, made from black Tournai marble, has been traced to twelfth-century Belgium and is believed to have come from the Castle Chapel. The tower dates back to the fourteenth century but the rest of the church was rebuilt in 1854.

Another church of note is the Methodist Church of Christchurch that greets visitors approaching from the south-east. Though the building in its current form dates back only to 1910, its soaring archway, crenulated tower and adjoining Masonic Hall are an impressive sight to greet visitors entering the town along New Road.

Mop Fair

FAIRS, MARKETS AND FESTIVALS

Saturday and Wednesdays are market day in Marlborough, but the Saturday market is displaced twice a year by a European Market, and also by a number of festivals that take place in the town.

The most dramatic festival is the annual Mop Fair that takes place in the autumn. This was traditionally a hiring fair that brought in employers and workers from the surrounding villages and dates back to the days where domestic staff and agricultural workers were taken on from one October to the next. Single staff would be hired for a year, provided with board and lodging and paid at the end. Prospective workers would bring in tools that marked out their particular skills; shepherds might carry a crook or a tuft of wool, dairymaids a pail or a milking stool, while housemaids might carry a broom or mop – hence Mop Fair.

It is easy to imagine that single workers receiving their first independent cash at the end of a year's work would choose to celebrate. Over the years, the Mop Fairs have developed into huge feasts, with a glowing reputation for infamy and excess. Even as the feudal society faded with industrialisation, the rural economy continued to hire in this way and the fair continued.

These days, the Marlborough Mop has little to do with getting a job and is more a last hurrah before autumn sets into winter.

> Twice weekly markets
> have taken place
> for over 800 years.

Though other fairs come to the town, they usually take place on the Common north of the town, elevated and invisible from the High Street below. The Mop sees the entire High Street taken over by a mechanised funfair for the two nearest Saturdays to Old Michaelmas Day, the 11th of October. Usually, these are consecutive but it's not allowed to take place on Old Michaelmas Day itself, so if this happens to be on the 11th, the Mops are spaced two weeks apart. Through traffic is suspended and the buildings of the High Street are dwarfed by massive rides covered in lights, each blaring out music from large speaker systems. The Mop Fair is noisy, exuberant and fun.

The Marlborough Jazz Festival, that runs over a long weekend in July, is the town's most significant cultural event running. This too displaces the Saturday Market. The Jazz Festival attracts leading musicians from

across the country and abroad, who perform in various pubs, halls and marquees around the town. Admittance is by 'stroller' tickets that are valid by day rather than for individual performances. This encourages an easy atmosphere where the audience can drift around the town and use their ears to choose the venues that are hosting the music that best suits their taste.

In September, the town also plays host to a Literary Festival that brings leading authors and writers to give talks and readings. This is less well-established than the Jazz Festival but, in a town that has produced authors such as William Golding, Sir John Betjeman, Dick King-Smith and many more, this is likely to grow.

Jazz Festival

WHITE HORSE

Wiltshire is known for its chalk hill carvings, and has the highest density of this art form in the world. The rolling chalk downland is ideal for such carvings; when the turf is cleared away the underlying chalk shines white, clearly visible from miles away. The most common image carved is the horse, a powerful Celtic symbol of strength, power and fertility. The white horses of today, however, don't date back nearly so far; in the nineteenth century, there was a positive fashion for hill art.

Though it sounds simple in principle, in practice it takes considerable sophistication to get hill carvings to look realistic. The viewer's perspective is very different from the carver's, and undulations in the ground add further complications. The Marlborough White Horse, being quite close to the town and easy to reach on foot, provides a great

This is Wiltshire's smallest white horse.

opportunity to take a close look at the terrain and appreciate the work involved.

It was carved into Granham Hill in 1804, probably to commemorate 600 years of the town's Royal Charter. The horse was designed by a student at Mr Greasley's School, then operating from Ivy House, now used as a boarding house by the College. He, along with his classmates, etched the horse into the slopes above the town. It is somewhat ironic that this local landmark is now only clearly seen from the grounds of Marlborough College. To examine it more closely, take the footpath that extends west from Granham Close on the south side of the Kennet; stay on the lower path for views of the horse or bear left up the hill to take a closer look. It's not clearly signposted but neither is it hard to find.

White Horse

River Kennet

THE RIVER KENNET

The source of the River Kennet is right by Silbury Hill, where water bubbles up from the ground at Swallowhead Springs. In the few miles to Marlborough, it is strengthened by further springs so by the time it runs through the town, the Kennet is already a substantial watercourse.

It is easy to see how this part of the River Kennet should have inspired our early Neolithic ancestors. There are very few temperate chalk streams in the world and they are always valued for their cool, clear and clean waters.

Through the seventeenth century, the river would have been lined with water meadows and there are several places where you can get a scent of this rural past. To the west, Preshute Church is beautifully set on the banks above the river before it spreads into the ponds of Treacle

Bolly; Cooper's Meadow in the heart of town is a classic floodplain, still grazed by sheep; and to the east at Stonebridge Meadow. From there, the river heads out to join the Thames.

Most of the upper Kennet has been designated a Site of Special Scientific Interest (SSSI) and information boards along its route indicate local resident wildlife.

The mills that once lined the Kennet in Marlborough, as it divides round the islands of Foley and Town Mill, have now been replaced by retirement homes and sheltered housing. Undisturbed by industry, the Kennet today wriggles unobtrusively through the town and even with today's population pressures, the water still looks clean enough to drink.

> Many rare species including otters have been spotted in the Kennet around Marlborough.

Avebury Stone Circle

AROUND MARLBOROUGH

As a centre for the earliest civilisation, the Marlborough area is particularly rich with echoes from mankind's distant past. Devil's Den is about two miles west of Marlborough, an atmospheric funerary structure where a huge sarsen stone balances on two uprights. The Neolithic tomb known as West Kennet Long Barrow is four miles west of Marlborough and is signposted from the A4; it's a short walk from the road. A mile further and you can hardly miss the mound of Silbury Hill, the largest Neolithic structure in Europe. It's no longer possible to climb it but it's right by the road. Another mile – and a right hand turn – reaches the huge henge at Avebury. This in many ways rivals Stonehenge, itself only 40 minutes away by car, but is a far more

relaxing site to visit. At Avebury, it is possible to wander freely amongst the standing sarsen stones and soak up the atmosphere of an unimaginably distant past.

Eight miles to the south-east of Marlborough are a couple of outstanding relics from a more recent past that are well worth a visit in the summer. In the village of Wilton, there is the only working windmill in Wessex. This still produces wholemeal, stone-ground flour and offers guided tours on Sundays and Bank Holidays between 2pm and 5pm from Easter to the end of September. A few fields away in Crofton, though rather further by road, is a huge brick chimney that towers over the world's oldest working steam-powered beam engine still performing its original function. This 200-year-old Boulton and Watt steam engine was built to pump water up from the Kennet to fill the canal. This fine example of industrial archaeology is still fired up occasionally on special steaming weekends, while the café is open from Easter to the end of September.

The south-east of Marlborough is cradled by Savernake Forest. This once stretched all the way to Hungerford and covered 150 square miles, and even now is the largest privately-owned forest in the UK.

A number of Savernake trees would certainly have been alive at the time of the Norman invasion. One such is the Big Bellied Oak that is four miles south of Marlborough on the Salisbury Road, with a girth of 11 metres at its base. To say you can't miss it doesn't quite do its situation justice as it almost protrudes into the road; in a car heading south it's important that you do. The

Avebury World Heritage Site lies six miles to the west of Marlborough.

most significant trees are named; each is different and has its own character. In the eighteenth century, Lancelot 'Capability' Brown was hired to landscape the forest; huge avenues of beech were planted but few of those trees remain.

Less ancient sights include the White Horses carved into the chalk hills of the area. Marlborough has its own but there are seven more close by. Summer visitors might want to track down each year's selection of crop circles; this part of the country is known for them though it's hotly contested whether this is because of ley lines converging on Avebury or its proximity to the Barge Inn at Honeystreet. If there's no easy vantage point, it is possible to hire a microlight for an aerial view.

Wilton Windmill

© geogphotos / Alamy

THE STATUTES OF MARLBOROUGH 1267 HENRY III.
An Act of Parliament passed in the Great Hall of Marlborough Castle near this place. "He made many statutes for the betterment of his realm and the manifestation of Common Justice".
Location: Marlborough College Main Gate

THOMAS WOLSEY
1473 - 1530.
Cardinal Archbishop of York and Lord Chancellor of England. Ordained Priest in this Church 10th March 1498.
Location: St Peter's Church

LORD CHAMBERLAIN'S MEN - SHAKESPEARE'S COMPANY.
Performed in the courtyard of the White Hart through the archway in the 1590's "All the world's a stage"
Location: 114 High St

EGLANTYNE MARY JEBB 1876 - 1928
Founder of Save the Children Fund taught in this building when it was St Peter's School.
Location: 91 High St

BATTLE OF MARLBOROUGH 5TH DECEMBER 1642.
Near this place a Royalist Army fought their way into the Town and defeated the Parliamentary Garrison.
Location: Castle & Ball Inn

THE GREAT FIRE OF MARLBOROUGH 28TH APRIL 1653.
Began near this place, at the house of Francis Freeman, Tanner "Where in three hours were consumed at least 250 houses".
Location: 48 High St

THOMAS HANCOCK 1786 - 1865.
Inventor of the vulcanisation of rubber.
WALTER HANCOCK 1799 - 1865.
Inventor of the Passenger Steam Road Carriage lived here.
Location: 3 High St

SAMUEL PEPYS DIARIST 1633 - 1703
'... lay at the Hart a good house and there a fair and pretty town ..." on 15th - 16th June 1668. Parts of the inn's galleries remain in nearby buildings.
Location: 114 High St

WILLIAM GOLDING 1911 - 1993
Author and Nobel Literature Laureate lived in this house - "Our house was on the Green, that close-like square, tilted south"
Location: 29 The Green